Robin & Wolf Sella

Through
the
Mourning Mist

Also by Holly Snow Sillau

Robin's Wings (2011), coauthored by Robin Joy Sillau

Missing Robin (2012)

In Robin's Voice (2013)

These books are available on amazon.com.

Through the Mourning Mist

365 Poems of Validation and Encouragement

Holly Snow Sillau,
Robin's mom

Printed via CreateSpace

Published in the United States of America
19 18 17 16 15 14   1 2 3 4 5

ISBN-10: 149483861-3
ISBN-13: 978-149483861-4

Printed via CreateSpace
First printing: 2014

E-mail the author: Holly.Sillau@gmail.com

Layout design: Kimberly Martin
Back cover photo: Lesley Unruh and Steve Mallin
Front cover photo: JPL Designs

As always—
for
Robin,
1984 – 2010

Contents

Acknowledgments ix

Introduction 3

The Poems 7

Giving in Robin's Memory .373

About the Author 375

Acknowledgments

To those who have helped me,
I want to give my thanks in verse,
And I think I'll start with a close chum first.
To read each poem and to encourage me was her plan,
So I say a hearty thank you
to Mrs. Dillingham—my good friend Nan.

When clouds of grief would fill my day,
There's a person who always knew the right things to say.
She offered me some helpful criticism,
And she opened the doors to a wealth of optimism.
She has the ability to capture sunshine's every ray.
Many thanks go to my sister,
my very best friend—Mrs. Shackelford, Barbara J.

And now—to the woman forever young
who still inspires my world,
All my thanks and love go to Robin Joy—
my radiant angel, my sweet little girl.

Through
the
Mourning Mist

Introduction

My daughter, Robin, was my only child, and I raised her alone. She passed away unexpectedly in January of 2010. She was twenty-five years old and had suffered from undifferentiated connective tissue disease—a painful rheumatological disorder—with symptoms emerging when she was only about eleven. I established a memorial research fund at New York City's Hospital for Special Surgery so that Robin's doctor, Dr. Lisa Sammaritano, could try to discover more about Robin's illness and other autoimmune diseases like it. All proceeds from the sale of my four books (*Robin's Wings: Lessons from My Daughter on How to Grieve for My Only Child; Missing Robin: Poems from a Mother's Grief Journey* [some of the poems in the book you are holding in your hand come from others that first appeared in *Missing Robin*]; *In Robin's Voice*; and *Through the Mourning Mist: 365 Poems of Validation and Encouragement*) go to the fund.

Robin was an interior designer in New York City, and she kept an online blog in which she wrote mostly about her work. She'd talk about furniture, carpeting, wallpaper, paint colors, and the like, but from time to time, she would write pieces about how she handled her ailment. In an entry from 2009, Robin wrote that she'd have given anything to have had something to read to let her know she wasn't alone on her path of illness. It was that blog entry that inspired me to write *Through the Mourning Mist.* I chose to write quatrains (four-line poems) because I wanted to make one helpful point in each piece, and I decided that a short poem would fit well into that plan. The earlier verses offer validation for the feelings experienced by bereaved parents. Each of the later ones offers its own bit of encouragement as grief progresses.

The poems transition slowly from descriptions of the pain felt by those suffering the loss of a child to how others treat us. They go on to words of comfort and hope. You'll find that some of the themes appear several times. That's due to the cyclical waves of grief that normally occur.

It's important that you read the quatrains in order and that you read only one each day. In this manner, I hope that, for a year at least, you'll feel supported by and accompanied by someone with whom you can identify as we continue together on grief's endless journey.

No matter how far apart from you
your former friends have grown,
I'm here to tell you that you needn't grieve alone.
As we linger at the rim
of grief's many emotional canyons,
We'll face the future together
as empathetic and understanding companions.

Holly Snow Sillau

1

Hankies wet and worn.
Hearts ripped and torn.
Parents sad and forlorn.
Fellow grievers, together let us mourn.

2

No more sensations—not a one.
My life might as well be considered done.
Nary a clock's tick, nary a tock—
I feel nothing because I am frozen in shock.

3

I can only sob, and I can only weep.
The ache in my heart is there for keeps.
My sense of loss is so frighteningly deep
That I can no longer eat,
and I can no longer sleep.

4

The thought of being without her pricks me
with a million syringes
While on every aspect of my life,
this grief always impinges.
There are horrible days lying ahead that I know
can be anticipated
As I consider the terrifyingly anguish-filled
future for which I am sadly fated.

5

Is there an end to this tunnel? Will I ever
see light?
So far, there's been only sadness with no hope
in sight.
The pain is so strong and unbearably
excruciating
That my will to go on is rapidly disintegrating.

6

These feelings of grief are nearly impossible
to explain.
Sometimes I feel as if I'm going insane,
And as I mentally wander from pillar to post,
It's the anguish from losing her
that stings me the most.

7

Feelings unexpected.
Future undirected.
Normalcy unprotected.
Both body and soul affected.

8

These twenty-four hours combine
to make a terribly challenging day.
I remember her birth, her death's anniversary,
other special times—all painfully gray.
No matter the significance
of any particular commemoration,
Each slices, impales, and inflames—
such a hateful abomination.

9

Because I love my lost child
more than any individual words can say,
This pain is the greatest price I can ever pay.
As I mourn her passing,
I have embraced one belief:
With such a staggering piercing of my heart,
this is the worst possible grief.

10

As I turn through my life's current pages,
And I find myself in grief's early stages,
My heart and my mind
have become quite unstable
Because to accept this loss,
I am completely unable.

1 1

Grief cuts, grief stings,
and makes my life unsteady
As would the damage from the blade
of a sharpened machete.
With pain coming in waves
and coming in spurts,
Every single part of me hurts.

12

My feelings lately I cannot control.
They rise up from the innermost reaches
of my soul.
With incendiary fury
and some raucous clangor,
Venom fills me full of anguish
and seething anger.

13

This could never have happened—
something so vile.
It's worse than any other misfortune or trial.
Tending to put my grief into perpetual exile,
I just can't believe it's true—
soothing denial, denial.

14

Forever apart.
Pain out of control.
I've lost my heart,
And I've lost my soul.

15

Even when I'm in a crowd
That's full of people noisy and extremely loud,
I still remain especially prone
To feeling completely lost and quite alone.

16

Since the day my world
took that terrible turn—
And my every circumstance became dire—
The pain in my heart has continued to churn
Within grief's searing and raging fire.

17

I often find myself unable to cope
When oppressed with so much despair.
I feel as if I have lost all hope,
And grief prevents me
from breathing in any air.

18

Now that everything in the world has changed,
Will I be able my life to rearrange?
Since I'll always be without her,
I've no idea how to start,
And I can't figure out how to deal
with this hole in my heart.

19

I'm gladdened by many of her personal things
Because around them, her aura always clings,
But the presence of her absence
leaves me mortified,
And the absence of her presence
leaves me horrified.

20

A gaping wound.
Raw exposure.
Heart harpooned.
No foreseeable closure.

2 1

As I stand by her grave on this spot
of sacred ground,
I feel as though my life has lost all its worth.
I can picture only my darling child
lying under that mound,
And I find myself doubting God's reasons
and the kindness of Mother Earth.

.

22

I cannot feel without my intact heart.
I cannot breathe when from my child,
I will always be apart.
I cannot walk without my feet.
I cannot live my life forever incomplete.

2 3

I have no trouble weeping
Since I'm tortured by grief and aching.
I've discovered that there is no sleeping,
And I'm almost always in a state of waking.

24

Her future was to be a lovely serenade,
But smashed were all the plans we made.
My heart and soul
are now injured and battered.
Her hopes and dreams
are now buried and shattered.

25

With this grief, will I forever be unable to deal?
Subject to this grief, will I forever be rejecting
what's now so painfully real?
Because of this grief, will I forever
be forced my feelings to conceal?
From this grief, will I forever
be powerless to heal?

26

I have trouble keeping my composure
As I strive to discover if there's some kind
of closure,
But my grief's agony continues to be brutal,
And my efforts—so far—
have been totally futile.

27

Cut down in her prime.
No reason, no rhyme.
Progression of time.
Grueling hurdles to climb.

28

I'm unable to find any peace or refuge
Since I'm drowning in tears from the loss
of my daughter.
Constant grief and pain cover me with waves
that are huge
As I sink below the surface
of all that foul water.

29

When into the future, I peer with sad eyes,
Through the darkness, I've come to realize
That grief's aching governs me
at my life's helm,
And I find that I've become
totally overwhelmed.

3 0

I used to experience emotions
in their full range,
But then she died, and everything changed.
Now I exist in one solitary mood.
Now I just sit around
and do nothing but brood.

31

It's been so long since I've smiled.
I can't—now that I've lost my child.
The pain is always present,
and if I had my druthers,
I'd want God to ensure that there'd be
no more bereaved mothers.

3 2

Why is she gone? There's no logic,
and I find no reason
With each year that passes
and with each changing season.
My life's normalcy has been thrown
by the wayside
As I stand here broken
at my precious child's graveside.

3 3

I ache because I miss my daughter.
I cannot breathe—I'm a fish out of water.
I love her more than words can render,
And for that love—to grief, I must surrender.

3 4

Who would expect such a wrenching change?
Everything is so peculiar,
and everything is so strange.
Life's now a hot and scorching red flame,
And not one single thing will ever be the same.

3 5

Soul bared.
Always scared.
No happy noise.
Life with no joys.

36

Where is my once-whole heart?
Where is my safe and comfortable home?
Where is my life's most important part?
They are all unfindable—
no matter where I roam.

37

My mind remembers only the pain.

My life is filled solely with grief and frigid rain.

My heart has been punctured

by an icy splinter—

These are my days in the midst of winter.

38

When the flowers begin to unfold,
Others feel joyful, but I feel downcast and cold.
The buds of spring depress and sadden me.
There's nothing left in this world to uplift
or to gladden me.

3 9

The season's heat reminds me of her zest
for being alive.
She'd never accept defeat, and that made her
larger than life.
To suffering, I am no longer a newcomer,
But oh, how I ache for her
in the dog days of summer.

40

Golds and yellows and reds turning brown,
The trees lose their mantle,
and my spirits go down.
Will I make it through autumn
watching the dead leaves fall?
Aren't these the cruelest reminders of all?

41

Flowers unplanted, hopes destroyed.
Wishes ungranted, plans null and void.
Altered souls, altered themes.
No more goals, no more dreams.

42

How shall I record her life etched into eternity
Upon a lovely granite block at her grave
for all to see?
What prayers shall I tearfully intone
As I think of what I ought to have engraved
upon that melancholy stone?

43

Maybe you think my aching and misery
ought to be hidden,
But I find that this agony always comes
unbidden,
And I don't understand why fate would allow
My loving home to be empty now.

44

I try to be joyful, happy, and light,
But you've no idea how I cry at night.
Though my grief my daytime demeanor
conceals,
I live with a wound that just never heals.

4 5

I have a nagging question that my grief
has brought on
As my tolerance for this uncertainty
wears thin.
Now that my only child is gone,
How can the earth continue to spin?

46

As I crouch down by her gravestone,
Mourning the greatest loss I have ever known,
To terrible pain and horror, I am prone,
Yet I continue to crouch down here—
all alone, all alone.

47

I agonize in grief as many thoughts close in.
I agonize over what could have been.
I agonize over what would have been.
I agonize over what should have been.

4 8

I am unable to appreciate the colors
found in nature's display.
They've all vanished from the lovely spectrum's
usual array.
Whatever I see is dull, and nothing has light.
She's gone, and everything shows up now
in only black and white.

49

No new paths or trails.
No new awards or glories.
No new adventures or tales.
No new heartwarming stories.

50

Why is she gone too soon? In German,
I can ask why with *warum*.
Why from me was she suddenly taken away?
In Italian, I can ask why with *perché*.
Why of this pain will I never be rid? In Latin,
I can ask why with *quid*.
With so many ways to ask for reasons why,
can anyone tell me why she had to die?

51

As into grief's dark pit I sink,
I lose my capability to think.
My usual levelheadedness begins to wane
Because my logical mind
is destroyed by my pain.

52

Who would ever expect such a twist?
Who'd ever believe this torment could exist?
From grief's cup, I've had to drink
the undrinkable,
And my view of life now sadly includes
the unthinkable.

5 3

Beethoven learned to make his way
through life without the use of his ears,
And he was able to write beautiful music
even though he couldn't hear,
But how will I be able to take another breath
After having lost my daughter
to eternity and to death?

54

I care about nothing, and I feel so numb
As I drift aimlessly through life's rough sea.
I wonder what she would have become,
And I'm afraid of what will become of me.

55

What once was joyous and bright
Now causes only anguish and fright.
From her passing, my thoughts never deviate.
Will grief's emptiness ever be able to dissipate?

56

Empty room.
No flowers in bloom.
Depression and gloom.
Forever, I presume.

57

My psyche's been fire branded.
My heart's been roughly sanded.
No one lets me be candid—
Abandoned by those afraid to understand it.

58

She wanted to get married and take care of me
as I grew old,
And there were so many good things left in life
for her to behold.
I know that I can look at no more new
photographs,
And I realize that we make lots of plans
while God simply laughs.

Based on a Yiddish proverb

5 9

I suffer daily, my heart filled with sorrows,
Because my beautiful child has no more
tomorrows.
She and I have paid the ultimate cost
Since my pain is caused by her young life lost.

60

All her friends are proceeding with their lives.
They're getting married,
and they're becoming wives,
But my daughter is unable to move on—
Now that she's dead, buried, and gone.

61

As my feelings of grief and anguish run wild,
I suffer many troubles and tribulations.
Not only do I mourn the loss of my only child—
I also mourn the death of my expectations.

62

The hard reality of this torment
never seems to morph
Since my heart is always yearning
for that binding tether.
According to American philosopher
Nicholas Wolterstorff,
On holidays, when the family is side by side,
we're not *truly* all together.

6 3

English poet Tennyson described rather well
How hard it is in my nightmare to dwell.
He wrote that one's words do the truth
half conceal
While those words can the truth merely
half reveal.

64

As the calendar pages turn,
My soul never ceases to burn.
For her presence, I continue to yearn.
Is acceptance a skill I'll ever be able to learn?

65

Everything is awry,
And nothing's in tune.
There are no reasons why
My child had to leave this world too soon.

66

My memories of her are rarely told.
Without her, I ache as I continue to grow old.
She is no longer vibrant and no longer alive.
My sweet daughter will forever be
but twenty-five.

67

I've cried for months, drowning in despair,
Reaching out for her in my dreams,
but she just isn't there.
I still can't believe that this deluge of tears
will end,
And I can't fathom living without her,
my only child, my very best friend.

From the poem "Laughter" by Holly Snow Sillau

68

Altered is my point of view.

Calm days are far between and few.

Grief is the one to blame,

And absolutely nothing will ever be the same.

6 9

Once grief's sharp teeth have bitten,
You'll be ever heartbroken as you deal
with the strife.
As English author Julian Barnes
had once written,
You remain tarred and feathered for life.

70

Into this grief, I have been suddenly flung
While I wonder why my daughter
had to die so young.
Since the number of her days
can no longer grow,
Tell me—what's wrong
with this hideous tableau?

7 1

My child has no future, and my heart is hollow.
There's no clear path before me,
and I've no directions to follow.
I'm lost in an angry cesspool, and I feel adrift.
Will this go on forever,
or will my spirits one day lift?

7 2

You see me grieve as you watch
from the outside,
And I know you haven't a clue,
But I'm in agony, here on the inside,
With no way to explain any of it to you.

73

This grief is the most terrible form
of purgatory—
Made worse by you demanding
that I keep private my agonizing story.
I'm all alone trying to manage
my everlasting despair
As I stand here by myself—
in the middle of absolutely nowhere.

74

I can't remember how to function,
and I cannot walk.
I can't remember how to think,
and I cannot talk,
So please don't criticize me
until after *your* child's untimely death—
Provided *you* can still recall
how to take even a single breath.

7 5

When your eyes gaze straight toward me,
You become uncomfortable in your skin.
Of my presence, you long to be completely free,
But is human kindness really
such a mortal sin?

76

Grief's hell cuts through me
like a very sharp knife,
And I'm sure nothing will ever be the same,
But I need to know that you remember her life,
So please don't be afraid to mention her name.

From the poem "Mention Her Name"
by Holly Snow Sillau

7 7

Please don't tell me that she's in a better place.
The place she belongs is right here, alive,
and with me,
And since there is no such thing
as grief's proper pace,
Don't tell me how long my challenging path
ought to be.

From the poem "Simple Requests"
by Holly Snow Sillau

78

Please don't tell me that this must certainly be
God's will.
God would never strike her down and cause me
this horrid pain,
And since my tears will always continue
to spill,
Don't tell me that my grief is time spent
in vain.

From the poem "Simple Requests"
by Holly Snow Sillau

79

Please don't tell me there's a good reason
for everything.
Some things go without any reasons why,
And since the fire of my lament
will always burn with flames that cling,
Don't tell me exactly how
you think I should get by.

From the poem "Simple Requests"
by Holly Snow Sillau

8 0

Tell me you're sad that I must endure such
an aching,
And show me that you're near even though I'm
terribly stressed.
Be more willing to engage in giving rather than
in taking,
And if you're really my friend, you'll lovingly
honor these simple requests.

From the poem "Simple Requests"
by Holly Snow Sillau

81

You become ill at ease when you see me
crying and weak.
Your own comfort is all that you really seek.
You've lost human compassion from your heart
and from your brain,
But please remember that I'm the one
in greater pain.

82

You want me to hold my words of pain
unuttered
Even though they've been keeping my heart
completely cluttered.
I know you wish I'd bite my tongue
as my feelings you dismiss,
So I say to you, fair-weather friend,
"Won't you please bite this?"

8 3

As I walk aimlessly down the street,
In hopes of a kindred spirit perchance to meet,
You see me in pain,
and you don't know what to say,
So you quickly change your path
and rapidly run away.

84

Does an alcoholic ever recover?
Is an addict ever free?
Consider this bereaved mother—
Just what do you expect from me?

85

You're quick to criticize me,
And you're quick to analyze me,
But you're slow to understand
my heart's biggest bruise.
I wonder if you'd like to walk
a mile in my shoes.

86

You say you'd behave differently,
and when we meet, you sneer.
You tell me that you surely would have
better ways to do it,
But to paraphrase English writer
William Shakespeare,
Everyone can master a grief
but he who must go through it.

87

You want me to squash grief's heartfelt,
strong bellow.
You require me to be silent and meek,
But in the words of American poet
Henry Longfellow,
"There is no grief like the grief
that doesn't speak."

8 8

When my ear you are demanding,
My anguish only doubles,
So please don't offer understanding
By telling me *your* troubles.

89

About my altered demeanor,
you've sometimes complained,
But I hope, my friend, you'll ultimately believe
That as French writer Victor Hugo
once wrote and explained,
Grief changes those who grieve.

90

Perhaps you don't know what to do for me,
So your first reaction is to vanish and flee,
But please don't disappear and hide—
I need only to have you by my side.

9 1

Don't you remember from your days at school
That we were all taught to follow
the Golden Rule?
So why, as I grieve,
don't those words you pursue?
Why don't you do unto me
as you would have me do unto you?

92

You offer me words of mock erudition
Along with many a baseless admonition,
But I'd not be apt to believe my eyes
If *you*'d be able to do as you advise.

9 3

Don't tell me you know how hard it is
to see a loved one go
Just because your heart got broken last week
by your longtime beau.
Don't tell me you can understand
the reasons why I weep
Just because you recently had to put your
adorable pet to sleep.

94

The latest pictures of your kids
are what you love to advertise,
But I have no new photos to obtain.
I do, though, have loads of memories to prize,
And that helps me my sanity to retain.

95

I am like an alien—alone and exiled—
So with your advice, you make an appeal,
But unless you have also lost a child,
You have undeniably no idea how I feel.

96

As my sad face you are viewing,
And your curiosity begins to grow,
You ask me how I'm doing,
But do you really want to know?

97

You want me to leave grief behind
and get to what comes after.
You want to see me joyful again
and hear the sound of my laughter.
You want me not to harbor
the painful thoughts to which I often cling,
But I can readily assure you
that there just is no such thing.

9 8

Some festive days are more difficult
than others
For those with lost children—
for this bereaved mother.
At those special times of the year,
you cannot imagine how alone I feel,
But did you ever think of including *me*
at your holiday meal?

99

A woman whose heart was clearly made of ice
Once gave me some asinine, absurd advice.
It came out of nowhere
and certainly seemed wild.
She foolishly told me
never to think about my lost child.

1 0 0

You see me walking all alone
As I bear the worst grief I've ever known,
And just when we're about to meet,
You turn and quickly cross the street.

101

You've seen my life fall around me in ruins,
Yet you're afraid to say anything heartfelt
or real.
You think that maybe you'll reopen
my wounds,
But this gash of mine will never be able to heal.

1 0 2

In order to offer me means
for making some pain go away,
You've often recited to me a well-worn cliché.
I've tried hard to listen with respect
and with grace,
But if *there* is so much better,
would you like yours to be in that place?

103

You're quick to tell me I should not fret,
And you're quick to tell me I should forget.
You're quick to tell me I should move right on,
But how quickly would *you* run
grief's crushing marathon?

104

You try to distract me, but there's a snafu.
My pain your good intention just aggravates.
Where grief is fresh and grief is new,
Any attempt to divert it only irritates.

Based on a quote from English author
Samuel Johnson

105

No matter how bruising
someone's physical wounds may be,
It's emotional trauma that is the bigger deal
Because the scars you are unable to see
Are truly the hardest ones to heal.

1 0 6

Those of you who've never lived with grief
Often present to me your methods
for finding relief,
But your suggestions offer me no assistance
Because it's quite "easy to be brave—
from a safe distance."

Based on the writing
of ancient Greek fabulist Aesop

107

As I try the vast fields of grief to plow,
One thought runs through my head.
Though you tell me things will get better,
I don't see how
Because my child will still be dead.

108

I know you're watching to see how I'll behave,
And you're praying that I'll neither
rant nor rave,
But my torment is something
you're unable to see,
And it's all due to the grief that ever lives here
inside with me.

109

There's so much pain ahead
lasting many years long
Since to have seen her grave
is just plain wrong.
All my sensibilities have now been defiled
Because a mother's not supposed
to outlive her child.

110

I cannot believe all this has taken place,
And my original plans I can no longer embrace.
The pangs, the stings, the ultimate shocks—
This new life is so terribly unorthodox.

1 1 1

A widower is a man who has buried his wife.
A widow is a woman who has lost
her partner in life.
An orphan is a person whose mom and dad
are gone,
And me, a bereaved mother—
what moniker shall I fall back on?

112

My child's passing fills me with strife.
It's destroyed every single normal part
of my life.
I can't imagine how I'll ever find ways
To manage the hours of the rest of my days.

113

I despair now that we are apart.
My grief lives inside me and remains unspoken.
There's such sorrow that can be found
within my heart,
And my fragile spirit has been forever broken.

Based on a proverb from the Bible

1 1 4

The passing of my child is the worst thing that
ever could be,
So you try to help with some pleasant
conversation, and yet,
You fear that your words may somehow end up
reminding me,
But do you honestly believe that I can
ever forget?

1 1 5

I'm unable to think clearly,
And my logic has a failed motif.
I miss my child so dearly
That my powers of reasoning are unhinged
by my grief.

Based on a comment made
by Victorian English art critic John Ruskin

116

I've gained some knowledge
from French writer Voltaire
Now that my crying has become a daily affair.
Weeping does offer me a modicum of relief
Because "Tears are the silent language of grief."

117

I found an expressive and pointed quote.
Our common anger it did denote.
A deaf composer (in a letter) once wrote
That he wanted to seize fate by its very throat.

Based on a quote from German composer
Ludwig van Beethoven

118

Another day of weeping is finished.
Another night is over with sleep diminished.
Since she's been gone, the earth has not spun.
I feel this way, but am I the only one?

119

When my misery gets to be more
than I can bear,
I make a decision right there and then
Because in order to quell
my overwhelming despair,
I must repeat my grief story
over and over again.

Based on a quote from French author
Pierre Corneille

1 2 0

Don't tell me in which direction
my life should go.
Without experience, no one is a wise man.
Naturally my spirits are bound to be low,
And besides, I'm already dancing
as fast as I can.

121

I'm unable to think, and I don't recall how
to be.
I don't know how to feel, and I'm no longer me.
All the fibers of my life I must now reweave.
I must rediscover how to exist
and even how to breathe.

1 2 2

As I deal with my pain, my heart empty
and hollow,
Inexperienced counsel from others
I am unable to follow.
To those who judge my tears, I offer this plea—
Let me choose to grieve in ways
that work for me.

1 2 3

Something that's often worried me
And caused many anxious tears to drop
Is how I will manage and how things will be
The day the visiting casseroles stop.

1 2 4

I know all this grief makes you antsy
In the absence of healing words and
curative drugs,
But I don't need from you anything fancy.
All I need is the comforting warmth
of your hugs.

From the poem "Your Hugs"
by Holly Snow Sillau

125

As I scan through my dictionary
and through my thesaurus,
I find a litany of words in an infinite chorus.
No matter how many depictions
these books fully contain,
This grief is simply impossible to explain.

1 2 6

People tell me to get quickly past my grief.
My days of mourning they advise me
to keep private and brief,
But no matter what these others
may think or say,
I know that Rome surely was not built in a day.

127

I need to accept all the horror
that has occurred.
My pain and my agony must not be deferred.
To decrease the weight of this albatross,
I give myself permission to grieve
and to feel the loss.

128

My parents were confident I'd continue our line,
But with my only child's passing,
there will be no grandkids of mine.
No matter my pleas and no matter my prayers,
I will leave this world without any heirs.

129

Though in your eye a tear may glisten,
It's important to me for you to listen
As I talk about this grief that makes me weak,
So help me let it out—please let me speak.

130

As I grieve, you tell me
to move on and to forget,
But how callous and unfeeling
can you actually get?
This world can offer me no special magic wand
That can ever undo—between this
mother and child—our unbreakable bond.

131

I'm often asked how many children I've got,
And I used to wonder what I could say
that was clever.
Should I speak the truth, or should I not?
I *do* have one precious child—
though she's lost forever.

132

If your heart is barren and your spirit is cold,
If your comportment is always calm
and controlled,
If you don't feel sad when someone must leave,
Then you won't understand that because
I truly love, I deeply grieve.

133

You have made me feel alone, abandoned, and
shunned.
Your behavior has shocked me, and I'm sitting
here stunned.
For your cold absence of support, I can offer
you no pardon,
So I shall begin to remove the weeds
from my friendship garden.

134

Grief for my daughter makes me think
nothing's worthwhile,
And my reactions to this loss
are all running wild.
Such unique pain has its own special style,
But I do know that everyone
is somebody's child.

135

I'll depend on myself full blast—
Whom else have I really got?
I'm sure my grief will always last,
But your sympathy will not.

136

About my pain, I must be permitted to speak.
Some comfort from sharing
is what I must be allowed to seek.
If not, then much more agony will arise
Because unexpressed grief just multiplies.

137

Years before she passed, I'd been told
by many folks
That I was courageous and as strong
as a thousand sturdy oaks,
So I used to think that in difficult situations,
I'd be braver,
But as was stated long ago, grief teaches
even the steadiest minds to waver.

Based on a quote
from ancient Greek playwright Sophocles

138

As one year of grief turned into the next,
I spent that evening anguished and vexed.
While others were celebrating New Year's Eve,
I was agitating over why she'd had to leave.

139

As I stare in the mirror
at that grieving mom's reflection,
I tell myself how I might try
to minimize my dejection,
But wouldn't it be so wonderfully nice
If I were able to follow my own advice?

140

Judging from the look on your face,
you probably think I'm nuts.
You see me constantly ache, yet you're unaware
that for grief, there are no shortcuts.
I could try to describe for you this pain,
but I daren't
Because the only one who might understand is,
sadly, another bereaved parent.

141

I hesitate to put my pain away.
It keeps us tied together, I'm amazed to say.
Though I want to feel better,
I want us to stay close—I really do.
I want to have my grief,
and I want to eat it, too.

142

Do I seem at peace and eerily calm—
This once strong and able supermom?
Can you still recognize
the formerly unflappable me
Now that I'm besieged by the grief
you cannot see?

143

Most people mark the years with BC and AD,
But those are scales that no longer work well
for me.
I just have to put all convention aside
As I now measure time
from before and after she died.

144

I often well up with unshed tears.
I have no other means
by which to ease my fears.
Sometimes I try to squelch each sigh,
But I know now that it is really okay to cry.

145

Yesterday I walked forward
with a lightened tread,
But today it's progress I seem to lack.
Yesterday I moved a few inches ahead,
But today I moved a few inches back.

146

Here's something that needs to be said.
I'll tell you that for a bereaved mother,
I am doing well when I can get out of bed
And just put one foot in front of the other.

147

To keep you from feeling awkward or at sea
Really puts me to the test.
Being kinder to you than you are to me
Prevents me from finding any peace or rest.

148

I wonder how my lost daughter is doing today.
I wonder if my dead child is feeling okay.
Are these notions normal to have,
Or do they merely serve as a soothing salve?

149

I want my lost daughter right here with me,
And it's so hard to swallow what never can be.
Between reality and wishes,
where should I draw the line?
Beloved child, please give Mommy
a definite sign.

150

I saw a girl who had your beautiful eyes.
When I got close enough,
it wasn't you whom I'd recognized.
I saw a girl who had your kind of hair.
I ran straight toward her, but you weren't there.

151

From "her" to "hear," I just insert the letter *a,*
And then I can hear her lovingly say,
"Mommy, onto 'hear,' add the letter *t*
from the alphabet chart,"
And that enables me to hear her
with my aching heart.

152

I make grief's journey all alone.
My former buddies got scared,
and away they've flown.
On this path of sorrow
along which my way I wend,
I have yet to find one true and caring friend.

153

How can I describe my new world of grief
to you?
No matter what words I use,
not one of them will do.
Adjectives have become my adversaries
Because there exist none horrific enough
in any of my dictionaries.

154

My life's been struck
by grief's deafening thunder.
My dreams and hopes have all gone under.
Are my thoughts about strength and courage
a serious blunder?
For now, I can only sit here and wonder.

155

I'll never say that she did. I prefer to say
that she does.
I always say that she is. I will not say
that she was.
Even though to you, it may make no sense,
I'll continue to speak of her
using the present tense.

156

We're all about to give thanks and eat,
But my beloved child belongs in that
empty seat,
So into myself, I begin to retreat
As I realize that our table
will forever be incomplete.

157

As I lie in bed crying and never sleeping,
I recall a notion that often gets me
through the night.
I understand that I am weeping
For that which has been my delight.

Based on a quote from Lebanese-born author
Kahlil Gibran

158

People tried to comfort me by saying
That I'd be my old self again soon.
They told me that my grief
wouldn't long be staying,
But they also believed in the man in the moon.

159

They abandoned me in my time
of greatest need.
They offered not a kind word nor a kind deed,
So my old alleged pals I now choose
to do without,
And I hope to find some better chums
amid this friendship drought.

160

As I rant and scream and sink below
And shriek and lament and cry,
I wonder why it takes only a minute to say hello
And forever to say good-bye.

161

Talking is a helpful way to find some
needed relief
From the torment and agony that upon me
heavily weigh,
But the circle of people to whom I can speak
of my grief
Grows smaller with every passing day.

162

The black curtains of my life are drawn
With all hope for the future disintegrated.
Now that my beloved child is gone,
The world seems suddenly depopulated.

Based on a quote from French poet and politician
Alphonse de Lamartine

1 6 3

In my life, music once played a significant role.
You might even say it was the sound
of my soul,
But now it hurts my ears
and scrapes my throat
As I hear those same songs played
with drastically different notes.

164

A famous writer penned a useful line
That helps me manage this heartache of mine.
It's good for me to cry, bawl,
and shake like a leaf
Because "To weep is to make less
the depth of grief."

Based on a quote from English poet and playwright
William Shakespeare

165

I'll try not to wallow in my distress
While through my agony, I attempt to progress,
But as I travel grief's unpredictable track,
I take three steps forward and two steps back.

166

If this raging fire of grief
should ever burn down to a single ember,
It's not the thoughtless words
of my acquaintances that I shall remember.
What really stings and most offends
Is the deafening silence of my so-called friends.

This is the poem "Desertion" by Holly Snow Sillau.
It is based on a comment made by American pastor
and activist Dr. Martin Luther King Jr.

167

Why have I lived to see her buried?
This is an issue I've pondered and queried.
Our deaths will have happened
in the proper sequence's reverse—
Thus violating the normal order
of the entire universe.

168

Everything pertaining to me
has always been filed
Under "She's the mother of a lovely child,"
But since she has passed
with such a terrible cost,
My life's job and my identity
now have both been lost.

169

I'm working hard to become adjusted,
but recently I have found
That I cannot make my way on any ordinary
or steady ground.
As I try to progress on grief's unpaved street,
Horror pulls the rug out
from right under my feet.

170

It's my right to be supported—with my feelings
sanctioned and recognized.
It's my right to be consoled—with my heavy
heart acknowledged and legitimized.
I'll not hide my constant sadness,
but I will shine a light on my most painful grief
In hopes of obtaining some soothing and some
very well-deserved relief.

From the poem "License to Grieve"
by Holly Snow Sillau

171

Another day breaks at dawn
And from lack of sleep—a great big yawn.
When I can't imagine
how with today's grief I'll be doing,
I notice that—there on the counter—
my *mourning* coffee is brewing.

172

Before she died, lots of things got me upset,
But now for those same issues,
I currently think—"No sweat."
I pick my battles in ways more selective.
I'm able to see my life
with a totally new perspective.

173

A question mourners frequently ask
Involves exactly how to manage this
painful task,
But no matter your talents at being a planner,
Grief cannot be handled
in any one particular manner.

174

The WHY question—
no matter how often I ask it—
Has an answer found only inside her casket.
It's a query without any solution,
And for my resulting anguish,
there is no possible dilution.

175

Keep your memories, but hold not to the past
Since there's only one thing in life
that actually lasts.
As Greek philosopher Heraclitus
once clearly proclaimed,
There's nothing that ever endures but change.

176

When everything feels out of season,
The words of a wise man remind me
about grief and love.
The heart will always have its reasons
Which reason knows absolutely nothing of.

Based on the writing
of French mathematician and author Blaise Pascal

177

Once you face your terrible catastrophe,
An altered life will be a *fait accompli*.
I tell you this from experience
and from expert authorities.
Your values will change—
and so will your priorities.

178

Even though some others not bereaved
may offer a helping hand,
From the outside looking in,
those others can never understand,
And no matter how many descriptions
our portrayals contain,
From the inside looking out,
we with lost children can never explain.

179

We go through life expecting the usual
and the typical,
But fate has its own plan
and is most often fickle.
The hardest grief happens—
and I can assure you it's the worst—
When your precious child's life is over,
and she has died first.

180

No matter the way your child has died,
None of us can remain calm
and completely dry-eyed.
We are bound together by heartache
and other such links.
Our kids are gone, and it just plain stinks.

181

Your obstacles will surely get easier to climb,
And your loss will get lighter to bear with time.
In the midst of your days
most difficult and trying,
If someone tells you those things—they're lying.

182

When others don't know exactly what to say—
And having no idea of the price we pay—
They'll offer common platitudes as if they knew.
They'll say that time heals all wounds,
but it's just not true.

183

If you didn't love much,
You'd not long for your child's touch,
But when your love is boundless and strong,
You grieve all your life long.

184

You'll find that keeping quiet aggravates.
You'll learn that pretending to be calm agitates.
You'll see that ignoring your pain strangulates.
As Roman poet Ovid said,
"Suppressed grief suffocates."

185

Tears are not a sign of meekness.
Crying is not evidence of weakness.
Lamenting is not proof of mental distraction.
They are each, to grief,
just a normal human reaction.

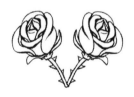

186

Against your grief, there can be no buffering,
And there are no protective punches
for you to pull.
I have learned that we can be healed
of a suffering
Only by experiencing it to the full.

Based on the writing of French author
Marcel Proust

187

A perceptive man said,
"Most of us are programmed to survive—
No matter how painful our losses may be."
We've got the inborn gumption
and the native drive,
So there's no need for us from our grief to flee.

Based on a quote from South African author
and psychiatrist Dr. Norman Rosenthal

188

Grief for your child is assuredly
the most complicated,
And it can never be fully
and completely articulated.
It's more intense than being
flung up against a brick wall,
And it's absolutely the most long-lasting grief
of all.

189

You say you want me to move past my pain,
And about my continued sadness,
you often complain.
When we're together, you become fidgety
and can't wait to leave,
But I'm going to take as much time
as I need to grieve.

190

My fellow bereaved parents, fate has picked us
To experience a pain so wrenching,
it's often beyond our control,
But as the English writer William Henley
reminds us in his poem "Invictus,"
"*I* am the captain of my soul."

191

What I—as I grieve for my child—
live daily is in its own special category,
And I need to discuss, describe,
and repeat my hideous horror story.
Though it's terribly difficult for me
to accept what I feel,
I know that talking about my pain will help me
to admit what is real.

192

To feel relief from my heartache,
it's hard to perceive
That some degree of peacefulness
I can somehow achieve,
But the best medicine for my pain,
I must believe,
Is to know that the only way
to move through this grief—is to grieve.

193

Will this loss always hurt so much?
Will I ever again near happiness' portal?
English poet Percy Shelley reminds me
with a thoughtful touch
That "Grief itself be mortal."

194

We are bound together by such special love,
And still grief assaults me
more than you can ever dream of,
Yet nothing can sever the cords that join
Since grief and love are opposite sides
of the very same coin.

195

The ties between my child and me, her mother,
Bind more tightly than any other.
Thank you, God, for giving me
your gift from above,
And thank you, God, for letting me experience
the greatest love.

196

It was always my lost child's personal view
That in difficult situations,
there are helpful things to do.
Against my misfortunes, I ought never to rebel
But rather *perstare et praestare*—
"to persevere and to excel."

197

I cannot be productive
if I live in a state of distress,
So I am resolved to move forward
and continue to progress.
My outlook will improve bit by bit
As I face my anguish and choose never to quit.

198

I need to make many a positive change
In order my world to rearrange.
To my different way of life, I must acclimate,
And new friendships I may need to cultivate.

199

This horror of mine is sure to last,
Yet I haven't lost all hope.
I know it's something I can never get past,
But I've elected to learn how to cope.

200

I must find a new way for coming and for going.
I must find a new way for understanding
and for knowing.
I must find a new way for breathing
and for seeing.
I must find a totally new way for living
and for being.

201

I won't go into hiding
or feel symptoms of withdrawal
Because there's a fundamental principle
I will always recall:
Even though I am in the most
painful condition,
Nothing can destroy me
without my permission.

Based on a quote
from First Lady Eleanor Roosevelt

202

Surrounded by rain and drenched in sorrow,
How can I go on to face tomorrow?
I'll think of her wit, and I'll remember her smile
Because no one can take from me
memories of my child.

203

When grief fills me up from my very core,
When my ice cold heart lies completely broken
on the floor,
When I think I can tolerate the pain no more,
I remember that the wings of my lost child
are here to help me soar.

204

Don't let quiet be the plan you devise
For reducing your unbearable chagrin.
It's not possible—and it isn't wise—
To remain silent or to shut your grief in.

205

I'll keep comforting thoughts around me,
And I'll let positive memories surround me
Because I'd be barking up the proverbial
wrong tree
If I were to let myself be bathed in negativity.

206

I'm down in the dumps with not one trace
of hope.
I prefer to sit around, to cry, and to mope,
But maybe I'll feel better if I engage
in activities constructive,
So I've decided to get out there
and do something productive.

207

Over my life, I feel that I've lost control
After the terrible loss living deep in my soul.
I may have to alter my future's primary plan,
But I must take charge of whatever I can.

208

This devastating misery
is horribly vast in scope,
And my broken life is hanging
by the last strand of a weak and flimsy rope.
Though with agony, doubt, and melancholy,
I must learn to cope,
I know my lost child would never want me
to lose even one little bit of hope.

209

As I maneuver through grief's
complicated maze,
There will be many obstacles I'll need
to surmount,
But I won't spend my time
counting all the painful days—
I prefer to try to make my precious days count.

210

I won't let my grief silence my voice.
I must make a determined
and proactive choice.
I must choose to succeed and to always thrive.
I must choose to live and to be alive.

211

If to ignore your sorrow is your helpful crutch,
You're asking for extra trouble
Because "If you suppress grief too much,
It can well redouble."

Based on the writing
of French author Molière

212

The chasm from infinite grief to living
is spanned by difficult growth,
And I know I'll require a healthy measure
of strength and courage both.
I am resolved to cross over from the first side
to the other
Even though from now on,
I'll be forever a childless mother.

213

The restless nights during which I find
myself awake
Work together to make me want to quit,
But my future is what I must now learn
to remake,
And into my life, my grief I must skillfully knit.

214

I'll manage the heartache
As I show my true grit.
I'll survive this emotional earthquake,
And I'll do so in spite of it!

2 1 5

My heart is broken,
and my routine has cracked,
But I must remind myself
of a most important fact:
Though the nights feel barren and empty,
and lonely are the days,
My child lives deep within me—
for now and for always.

216

My grief is painful, debilitating,
and always pulls me down
Into a sea of devastating hopelessness
where I seem to drown,
But our wonderfully constant tie
and our enduring mutual love
Are just what I need to make me smile
and to make me rise above.

217

How would I be able to make my way through?
I had no idea—not even a clue—
But somehow I realized that I actually knew
Exactly what my child would want me to do.

218

From her years of pain
as she dealt with her affliction,
And as I travel along my new path
covered with grief's scars,
I've learned to follow
my lost daughter's unalterable conviction:
Per aspera ad astra!—
"Through adversity to the stars!"

219

I have many moments when over my grief
I agonize,
So with my fellow bereaved parents,
I can surely empathize.
I do have a bit of advice I urge you all to utilize:
I always feel better whenever I exercise.

220

If you want to get back a ray of hope,
You must learn new ways to manage and cope.
Into your life, this grief you must weave,
So hesitate not—you must buck up and grieve.

221

This torment will forever last
Through pain-filled eons too numerous
to calculate,
Striking me with grief and aching
that I'll never get past,
But I must try to learn to accept it all
and thus—to acclimate.

2 2 2

As I drown in a sea where everything's amiss,
Thrust deeper and deeper
into grief's endless abyss,
What saves me is a lifeline
that must never be ignored:
There's love flowing both ways
through the eternal umbilical cord.

2 2 3

From now on, she'll hear the birds sing
by listening through my ears,
And the loveliness of life's beauty is what we'll
experience together for the rest of my years.
From now on, she'll see the rainbows
by looking through my eyes
Because ours is an unbreakable link
filled with love that never dies.

224

If and when I'll ever feel stronger,
there is no guarantee,
But I'm listening to one who's been there,
and I'm listening as carefully as can be.
I'm told that if I want to live again
and not just exist or only get by,
I've got to take good care of myself,
so with that edict, I will comply.

225

My child's voice I'll—of course—
forever long to hear.
I need to feel her life's music
broadcast loud and clear.
To not lose faith in my child's proximity,
I must continuously be on guard,
But I'll know she's near if I always listen closely
and if I always listen hard.

226

Courage is not the lack of fear.
It requires facing the grief that's always here.
I can be courageous—
though terror haunts me, I admit—
As I defiantly choose to leave fear behind
and move ever forward in spite of it.

From the poem "Courage"
by Holly Snow Sillau

2 2 7

When all the mournful thoughts within me
increasingly breed,
And I've actually no idea of what to do
or of how to proceed,
Of the many topics upon which I may elect
to cogitate,
It's the good memories upon which I must
choose to concentrate.

228

Grief's pangs cause me great desperation,
And these cruel circumstances
keep me from being free,
So when I am no longer able
to change the situation,
That's when I must go about trying
to change me.

Based on the writing of Austrian psychiatrist
and Holocaust survivor Viktor Frankl

229

I am under great duress,
Filled with grief and endless distress,
But I *will* go on, and I won't obsess
Because my courage is a trait
I will never suppress.

230

Of my child's presence,
I have recently been deprived,
But I realize that these last weeks and years,
I *have* survived.
I can still hear her voice,
and I can still hear her song,
And that's exactly what will help me
continue to be strong.

2 3 1

Grief has so many steep mountains to climb,
But I will conquer each peak just one at a time.
There are no easy exercises or repetitious drills,
Yet with effort, I hope to acquire
some helpful coping skills.

232

My future without her is now
so hard to envision.
For her loss, there is nothing
that can compensate,
But lately I've come to a helpful decision—
It's her cherished life that I'm choosing
to celebrate.

2 3 3

Sometimes my anguish makes me want
to tear out my hair
As I carry a pain much more than I can bear,
But the Roman philosopher Cicero
has made me aware
That grief would be no less if atop my head,
nothing were there.

2 3 4

Nothing's as binding as a mother's kiss,
And nothing can separate us—not even this,
So I'll repeat with each and every breath
That love is much, much stronger than death.

235

The nostalgic memories of her that I have today
Make me hurt and feel terrible sorrow,
But these same recollections
that now cause me dismay
Will become precious gifts tomorrow.

236

When I feel like I do not belong,
And I'm searching for someone to blame,
I know that I can make myself miserable
or strong,
And I realize that the amount of work involved
is really much the same.

Based on the writing of Peruvian author
Carlos Castañeda

2 3 7

When my heartache overwhelms me,
I recall something I need to do.
My common sense pointedly tells me
That I must accept my grief
and learn to live with it, too.

2 3 8

Though I am completely distraught,
Filled with grief and horror unsought,
I will remember all the joy she brought,
And I will be strong enough
to emphasize that lovely thought.

239

I realize that I need to have kindness
and serenity surround me,
So I'll try to look for some friends
who are brave enough to be around me.
I must seek out folks of a giving
and caring sort.
I need to find people who will offer me
true comfort and real support.

240

I can stay in bed and in so doing, opt
To behave as if my life has stopped,
But I'm sure my broken spirit I can revive
If I *choose* to stand up
and if I *choose* to survive.

241

My grief's problems I always juggle
In my effort to make a forward movement,
But if I never had to struggle,
There would be neither progress
nor improvement.

Based on the writing of African-American
social reformer Frederick Douglass

242

Her name on the list of the dead
makes me furious that I can't remove,
And there are so many other bitter issues
that I've got.
I know I should never be angry at what
I can improve—
Nor should I ever be angry
at that which I cannot.

Based on a quote
from Greek philosopher Plato

2 4 3

For my grief, I pay quite steeply,
But I know that my child's spirit will never flee
Because my daughter—whom I love so deeply—
Will always be an integral part of me.

Based on the writing of American author
and political activist Helen Keller

2 4 4

Having to bear all this painful stuff
Is as strange as if I came from Mars,
But when the sky is really dark enough,
I *can* see the brilliant stars.

Based on the writing of American historian
Charles Beard

245

I can choose to rise above my pain,
or I can choose to wallow in its debris.
I can choose to retire from living,
or I can choose to be the best that I can be.
I can choose to face my grief,
or I can choose to drown in its black hole.
I can choose to sit back and let things happen,
or I can choose to direct my heart and soul.

246

Sometimes my grief makes me angry
and tends to drive me mad.
It is, I'm sure, the most tortured pain
I've ever had,
But I must remember that not every aspect
of life causes me feelings that are bad,
So I will move forward with a normal
and healthy amount of sad.

247

I've been spending my nights and my days
all teary-eyed,
But I must let her strong and determined spirit
be my guide.
With her passing, I must try
not to be preoccupied.
I *will* be okay even though the fact remains
that my child has died.

248

I often sense that my unbearable sadness
ties me to my lost child,
So I tend to willingly slog through grief's ugly
heaps all around me piled,
But what I must really try to remember and
always try to think of
Is that what keeps us bound as one
is not the sadness—it's our everlasting love.

249

As I navigate grief's tumultuous sea
And climb its ever-looming hill,
If I don't take good care of me,
Then exactly just who will?

From the poem "Who Will?"
by Holly Snow Sillau

250

I have discovered a way
to decrease grief's aching malaise
By learning to enjoy the flowers
from my memory bouquets.
What helps most to keep me smiling
and relatively calm
Is the comforting knowledge
that I will forever be her mom.

From the poem "Forever Her Mom"
by Holly Snow Sillau

251

Somehow your words don't reach me
When you say that the years
will make my grief depart.
Father Time will just have to teach me
How to live with this perpetual break
in my heart.

252

I cannot control the flow of this grief,
And I cannot control others
with their heartless proclivities,
But I have learned a way
to find some kind of relief
By controlling my own behavior
and my own activities.

253

My spirits seem always to be descending,
But I'll not let my broken heart
keep my fractured wings from mending.
I must find a way to let them once again
enable me to fly,
So I'll turn my efforts to this task,
and with all my might, I'll try.

254

I thought my days of being a mom were done.
I believed there were no tender jobs
left for me—exactly none—
So my heart and my thoughts
began to run wild,
But I am determined to find ways
to continue to parent my child.

2 5 5

While facing my grief, I've found this to be true:
For my suffering,
there is no helpful consolation,
But I won't let my plight describe me
or become my permanent view
Since it's up to me to define my own situation.

256

I've seen most of my former acquaintances
fall short,
So I'll seek out people ready to offer me
honest support.
I'll surround myself with those able my soul
to nourish
In order that I can once again live, breathe,
and flourish.

257

I have decided to obey my child's loving decree
As I choose to neither merely exist
nor barely survive.
I'll make my lost daughter
extremely proud of me.
Though she's sorely missed,
I've elected to push on and to thrive.

From the poem "To Thrive"
by Holly Snow Sillau

258

My daughter faced her illness and fears
With courage and determination,
So I'll wipe away most of my tears
As I emulate her strength without equivocation.

259

To keep a calm demeanor all the while
And to exhibit no signs of grief,
society requires me,
But through every daunting oppression
and every emotional trial,
It's my lost child's pure and endless love
that inspires me.

260

My tears are smoldering, and I bear great pain.
My life is empty with no joy, no light, just void.
My mind is wobbly,
and I think I'm going insane,
But I *am* still breathing, and therefore,
I will *not* allow myself to be destroyed.

2 6 1

There is no bond tighter than that
of child and mother—
Forever in communication with one another—
So I have found a way to dry many a tear.
When I listen with my heart,
my child's voice I can still hear.

262

For the rest of my days and my nights,
we'll continue to be apart,
And as I look to the future without her,
I feel so scared,
But I must remember her beautiful face
and her extremely kind heart,
And I must be thankful
for all that we have lovingly shared.

2 6 3

I have many things that still need to be done.
I must be productive
and maybe even grab a bit of fun.
Though I'm bombarded with the pangs
of mourning's strife,
I will *not* allow grief to keep me from my life.

264

At dealing with my loss,
I must become adept.
There are two choices I've come across—
I can go crazy, or I can learn to accept.

265

I feel like my heart's been cut out of me,
Yet I will still search for a restorative key.
I don't know if I've anything left inside to give,
But I have decided to find the courage to go on
and to continue to live.

266

I've been dealt more than my fair ration.
My body shakes, and my face is ashen.
Although I'm mourning,
and I'm really quite frightened,
I know that grief shared
is definitely grief lightened.

Based on the writing of American rabbi
and counselor Dr. Earl Grollman

2 6 7

I hurt, I cry, and I miss my child like crazy
As my taste for the outside world sours.
Then into my head pops a truth that
saves me—
A difficult day lasts only for twenty-four hours.

From the poem "Twenty-Four Hours"
by Holly Snow Sillau

268

With each painful moment that passes by,
I will concentrate and really try
To accept the heartache I cannot quell
As I learn to keep my life and my grief
simply parallel.

From the poem "A Truly Valuable Skill"
by Holly Snow Sillau

2 6 9

Here is a concept I try to use as a guide
As this volcano of grief I attempt to climb.
It will never be okay that my child has died,
But I'll be all right with acceptance and time.

270

My life was changed that horrible day
gone wrong,
But I try to remain courageous and strong.
As I struggle to do whatever it takes,
I must always remember that even iron breaks.

Based on the wisdom of Mississippi native
Mrs. Delphine Hawthorne

2 7 1

I cannot prevent my soul from crying,
So I must learn to bear the sorrow of her dying.
No matter the pain, no matter the strife,
I will *not* let my grief take over my life.

272

Along grief's perilous path,
I stumble and I crawl
Until I remember comforting words like those
from American orator Robert Ingersoll.
Hope sees a star,
and if I concentrate on listening,
Love will hear the gentle rustle
of her peaceful and precious wing.

273

I can drown,
Or I can swim along.
I can lie down,
Or I can rise up strong.

274

To help me get my trauma's chasm crossed,
I must pay homage to the wisdom
of American poet Robert Frost.
I've learned from one of his poems
how I can do it.
He taught me that the very best way to handle
my grief is to bravely march through it.

From the poem "Unavoidable"
by Holly Snow Sillau

275

The loss of my child is so terribly sad.
It makes me crumble,
and I feel unbelievably bad,
But just when my grief
seems to be driving me mad,
I find the strength I didn't even know I had.

276

To my loss, I'm not sure how to respond.
It's a grief I can never seem to get beyond,
But I will not let it eat me alive,
And I'll find productive ways
to keep afloat and survive.

277

From the gratifications of parenthood
am I now excluded?
Has the joy I can derive
from her life concluded?
Have my mothering responsibilities
come to an end?
NO, NO, and NO—on that, you can depend!

278

With torment, my every hour is rife,
And it's my tensions that I yearn to release,
So I'll make my grief only a part of my life
And not its centerpiece.

279

Experienced grievers have often made
this decree.
They've announced it to others,
and they've announced it to me.
I'm trying to believe them,
and I'm trying to use it.
They've told me that hope
will be my grief's best music.

280

I won't allow myself to remain immersed
in this awful strife,
So I will concentrate really hard
to try to find some way
To integrate my frightful grief
right into my life—
Without having to pretend
that everything is okay.

281

I read a quote with which I must agree.
It's a nugget of wisdom English poet
William Cowper taught to me.
My journey of suffering
I must be willing to begin
Because "Grief is itself a medicine."

282

I found some encouraging words
that I will paraphrase
Because they help me
with some of my difficult days.
When all I see before me
is darkness and bleakness,
I'm reminded that even the strongest
have their moments of weakness.

Based on a quote from German philosopher
Friedrich Nietzsche

283

Worse than any pain I may come across
Is the horrible ache
from my beloved child's loss,
But I will find comfort
in my special gift from above,
And I will continue to be ever so grateful
for our binding love.

284

Everything now seems horrid and bleak.
Feverish tears always run down my cheek,
But even when the absence of blue skies
gives me a scare,
I know that the sun is still sitting right there.

285

If my leg had been fractured,
I would still take a chance
To get right up and relearn how to dance.
Now that my heart is broken
with nothing more to give,
I will get right up and relearn how to live.

286

I can choose to spend my time in anguish.
I can choose to curse her fate
with blasphemous language.
I can choose to yearn for my former
peace of mind,
But I'd rather choose to relish
what she's left behind.

287

My hours are filled with introspection
and mad raves.
The thoughts I have are dark and grim,
But since my grief attacks me
in thunderous waves,
I must take a deep breath, jump in, and swim.

288

Until my last intake of breath,
I'll honor my child's memory—now—
after her death.
She taught me to be strong
and the fates to forgive,
So since *I* am alive, I am *determined* to live.

289

Often one day is too much to be borne.
Even one hour causes my heart to be torn.
Every minute carries more grief
with which to be reckoned,
So I'll just have to get by second by second.

290

Though my misery is great
and my heart is breaking,
I've realized that there's more to my life
than just the aching.
Something that I hope will never end
Is the supportive comfort
of my few remaining friends.

291

I miss her because I love her.
From this torment will I find no relief?
From this ache will I ever recover?
I need to remember that love lasts
so much longer than grief.

292

She's sending signals—
though it goes against my common sense—
And I've noticed that odd things
seem to happen a lot.
Do you think it's all a great big coincidence?
Well, I certainly prefer to think not!

293

In achieving my goals, I'll not accept defeat
Because though my heart is shattered,
it continues to beat.
I've decided to be more relaxed
and more forgiving.
In other words, I've decided to go on living.

294

It's really true and not a rumor
That there are many healing effects of humor,
So I smiled, and then I laughed,
And my sadness began to reduce by half.

295

I dreamed that with this grief,
my life had been adjourned,
But the words of French author Albert Camus
awoke me from my restless slumber.
"In the depths of winter, I finally learned
That within me,
there lay an invincible summer."

296

A Hebrew proverb from a bit of ancient lore
Has got my heart abuzz—
Say not in grief, "She is no more"
But in thankfulness that she was.

297

As I ponder words from one of the smartest
of humankind,
A comforting thought is brought to my mind.
My heart need not feel a constant void—
Because my child's life energy
cannot be destroyed.

Based on the writing of German-born physicist
Albert Einstein

298

As the new year turns into January
from last December,
I must try to stay calm,
and I must try to remember
That when I doubt if I can go on
tolerating grief's bitter pill,
I know that I certainly have, I certainly am,
and I certainly will.

299

My grief has controlled me,
But my heart's just told me
That my child is beside me
To strengthen and guide me.

3 0 0

There's a useful skill I will learn to employ.
If I didn't, it would truly be a crime.
I must become able to carry
my grief *and* some joy
All at the very same time.

3 0 1

When I think back on our days gone by,
I find it hard to keep my eyes
and my tissues dry.
Those pleasant memories seem
to stab me—causing feelings most vile—
But what hurts me today
may tomorrow make me smile.

3 0 2

For a sign of her presence,
I continue to pray and wish,
And I wonder if we will be together again
one day.
I'm told by English poet Shelley
(that's Percy Bysshe),
"That to divide is not to take away."

3 0 3

I may not expect each of life's
songs and dances,
Though as I've heard
while moving through this wild ride,
I cannot always control
external circumstances,
But I can always control what goes on inside.

Based on a quote from American author
and motivational speaker Dr. Wayne Dyer

304

If it's my vocabulary that I don't sift and clarify,
Surely the anguish will do me in,
So I must soon learn to say good-bye
To "what if," to "if only,"
and to "should have been."

305

We can no longer talk face to face,
And this I must accept with grace.
Since our connection has entered
a brand-new phase,
We just communicate now in different ways.

3 0 6

My daughter remains my anchor, my light,
and my sustaining force
Despite this horribly inconceivable twist
in life's course.
Yes, I miss her with an ache that pierces me
to the bone,
But while I treasure her and love her,
I will never be alone.

From the poem "Missing Robin"
by Holly Snow Sillau

307

When I feel like my life's lovely bubble
has burst—
And when my torment is at its absolute worst—
I remember that I really ought
To give myself permission
to think a pleasant thought.

308

To manage my bereavement,
I have few controls,
And my anguish is amassing,
But one of grief's most prominent goals
Is to accept the reality of her passing.

3 0 9

I've made a choice
To lift up my voice,
So I'll be thankful
that even in her illness' haze,
She took great pleasure in each of her days.

310

I can flounder in today's sorrow,
And I can muddle through life's ways,
But I'd rather try to be happy for tomorrow
Because of our glorious yesterdays.

311

Though grief upon my heart does trample,
I've developed a mighty compulsion
To use her life as my guiding example
For teaching myself a new way to function.

3 1 2

I can dwell on her life gone by,
And surely I can tear up and cry,
Or I can recall the good things all the while,
And surely I can cheer up and smile.

3 1 3

I heard a bereaved parent make this claim.
She believed it, and I think I also should.
She told me that life will never be the same,
But it can certainly still be good.

314

My days are filled with horror and dread
Because I cannot prevent the birds of sorrow
from flying over my head,
But no matter what style of tresses I wear,
I *can* prevent those birds
from making their nests in my hair.

Based on "The Birds of Sorrow"
by American poet Ron Schreiber
(that work itself based on a Chinese proverb)

315

I grieve for my child in many styles—
Some so complex that they make me flinch—
But I know that a trip of any number of miles
Must be traveled inch by inch.

316

To make it through this difficult day
And to get some grieving done,
Either I will find a practical way—
Or else I will create one.

Based on the writing of English poet
Sir Philip Sidney

317

As I wrestle with many a grim situation,
I will allow no defeat and no capitulation.
In one premise, my resolve is secure—
I will become as strong as the grief I endure.

318

Don't ever see me as a parent formerly bereaved
Because I am and always will be
in heartbreaking grief.
At sanity's edge, I'm constantly hovering,
But I'm a bereaved parent
who is ever recovering.

319

I live with grief's endless needles and pins,
Yet I know that mighty trees get strong
in the winds.
I feel like I'm always inside a farmer's
old beating thresher,
But I know that diamonds—by nature—
are made under pressure.

Based on a quote from American minister
and author Peter Marshall

320

Toward the pit of disconsolation, I edge
As I creep right up to its very ledge.
I tend to find myself on grief's abysmal brink,
But "Perhaps I am stronger than I think."

Based on a quote from Anglo-American author
Thomas Merton

3 2 1

I found a saying that
from the Bhagavad Gita comes.
It remains in my mind
where it constantly hums.
Its helpfulness and comfort will surely persist
Because "That which is real
cannot cease to exist."

3 2 2

I look way up at the brightest star,
And I know for sure that she isn't far.
I look way up at the shining moon,
And I know for sure that we can still commune.

3 2 3

My heart with grief is rife,
But I do recall an important notion—
Though death has ended her sadly short life,
Our connection continues
like the sea's constant motion.

324

My search for support has begun,
But to where have all the people run?
Hey out there, where can everyone be?
Well, I guess I'll just have to depend on me.

325

My ability to manage my grief I often did doubt,
And I wanted to spend time
covered up in my bed,
But then I realized that there is no way out—
There is only a way ahead.

Based on the writing of English priest
Father Michael Hollings

326

In facing my grief, I've made many a false start
Since I have no anchor to which I can tether,
But I know that I'm not really falling apart—
I am simply coming together.

Based on the writing of American pastor
and author Bob Deits

3 2 7

Others who've traveled
grief's precarious byways
Told me that though my pain weighs
over ten trillion tons,
Slowly but surely,
I'll have some more good days,
And they'll soon begin
to outnumber the terribly awful ones.

3 2 8

I've learned that I'm able
to decrease my desolation
If from my sweet child I take my cues.
She was, she is,
and she'll ever be my inspiration—
My daughter, my angel, my muse.

From the poem "My Muse"
by Holly Snow Sillau

329

Her example of strength has given me
a fighting chance
To face my grief
and courageously walk through it.
I shall not be defined
by my unexpected circumstance,
But I will be defined by my responses to it.

330

If mourning's hurricane winds
cannot be changed,
Then your dreams and plans
must be rearranged,
So when cruel fate pounds you
with grief's gusts and gales,
You must realign and adjust your sails.

Based on a quote from American musician
Jimmy Dean

3 3 1

As you grieve, there's a wise thing for you to do.
You must take care of your precious health,
And as my lost daughter
would certainly say to you,
Therein lies your wealth.

3 3 2

You may want to stay inside and remain inert,
I suppose,
Your tear-stained face never to disclose,
But you can help release your emotions
from their captivity
By increasing your amount
of daily physical activity.

3 3 3

Even though you feel like you've been
through the Blitz,
Remember that appreciating humor
has many health benefits.
Since you are the one you need to look after,
When you find something funny,
it's time for some laughter.

3 3 4

English statesman Winston Churchill once said
that to handle our troubles, we mustn't tarry.
We must face our demons
and all the pain we carry.
Remember that to keep
your blood calmly flowing,
If you're going through hell, just keep going.

335

Each of us grieves in our own personal ways
With whatever gets us by on all those
difficult days.
In order to settle on what best
helps you pull through,
As in *Hamlet* we're told,
"To thine own self be true."

From the poem "Individual Grief"
by Holly Snow Sillau

336

Remember when you're crying
and your heart is aching
That strength isn't measured
by how much you bear prior to breaking.
It will be reckoned by a concept unspoken.
It will be measured by how much you bear
after you're broken.

3 3 7

When an emotional hassle
your mind wants to revive—
And you feel quite full of aggravation—
Remember that "Conflict cannot survive
Without your participation."

Based on a quote from American author
and motivational speaker Dr. Wayne Dyer

338

Please don't let your troubles amass,
And please don't wallow in grief's horrible pain.
Remember that you shouldn't stand by while
you wait for your storms to pass.
You'll feel much better if you learn
how to dance in the rain.

Based on a quote from American author
Vivian Greene

339

Here's advice on how not to let
your morale corrode,
And it must be acted upon
by every bereaved mother:
Joy and pain *can* live
in the same human abode,
And neither should deny the other.

Based on the writing
of Chinese author Tan Neng

340

When you are to grief's pain resigned,
And you continue to suffer at great length,
Remember: "You have power over your mind,"
And in this, you will find your strength.

Based on a quote from Roman emperor
and philosopher Marcus Aurelius

341

The value of amity is blatantly clear
When your emotions are at stake
Because friendship doubles our joy
and our cheer
And divides our dismal heartache.

Based on a Swedish proverb

342

When grief remands you to life's lowest shelf—
And melancholy screams at you
in its loudest voice—
You can be miserable,
or you can motivate yourself.
It will always be your choice.

Based on a quote from American author
and motivational speaker Dr. Wayne Dyer

3 4 3

Set your sights on the most radiant star,
And you'll come upon a hope-filled reservoir.
Since she's passed,
I've learned one sure thing—
When loving hearts listen, the angels sing.

3 4 4

If you look to the future and feel great dread—
If it's strength and courage you lack—
Bear in mind that to know the road ahead,
You should ask those who are coming back.

Based on a Chinese proverb

3 4 5

As you mourn and as you grieve
While tears drip from your eye,
Understand that to live inside the hearts
our children leave
Means that our sons and daughters never die.

Based on a work by Scottish poet
Thomas Campbell

3 4 6

Today is your death's mournful anniversary,
And rather than crying all day,
I choose to spend it recalling fervently
How you would elate me in every possible way.

From the poem "Difficult Commemorations"
by Holly Snow Sillau

3 4 7

Today is May's time for honoring me,
your mother,
And rather than stumbling
with many sad missteps,
I choose to spend it loving you above all others,
And as I do, I can rise up
from out of the depths.

From the poem "Difficult Commemorations"
by Holly Snow Sillau

3 4 8

Today is the day to celebrate your birth,
And rather than punching walls by the fistful,
I choose to spend it remembering
your joyful mirth—
Even if it makes me ever so wistful.

From the poem "Difficult Commemorations"
by Holly Snow Sillau

349

It hit me like a bolt from the blue,
And I felt that you were near,
So just because I can't actually see you
Doesn't mean you aren't here.

350

I see your face in the twinkling of night.
I hear your voice in melodies lilting and light.
I feel your presence, my little lamb,
Because you are everywhere that I am.

3 5 1

Mommy, don't agonize over what is not,
And don't be concerned with what will not be.
You must be grateful
for the memories you've got,
And you must rejoice
in your loving thoughts of me.

352

When it's me you try to find,
listen to the ties that bind.
When you look for me in the stars above,
listen to our undying love.
When you feel that we're forever apart,
listen to your very own heart.
As you remit grief's exorbitant toll,
remember that I'm here, Mommy,
alive inside your soul.

3 5 3

Remember how strong I was? From whom
did I get that trait?
Remember how determined I was? Who taught
me to always aim for home plate?
Remember how brave I was? Just how
did that arise?
Go to the mirror, Mommy,
and look deep within your eyes.

354

Please don't let your life come
to a screeching halt.
Stop laying blame, and stop finding fault.
Mommy, I want you to live,
and I want you to be.
I want you to enjoy the world for yourself,
and I want you to enjoy it for me.

3 5 5

To gain strength and courage,
we must look fear in the face
Even if it surrounds us
everywhere and everyplace.
We must do that which we think we can't,
And we just might notice
that our fear gradually becomes scant.

Based on a quote
from First Lady Eleanor Roosevelt

356

Krishna, in the Bhagavad Gita,
tells us with words that are his
That from the truth, we must not flee.
We must always work with what actually is
And not with what we think it ought to be.

3 5 7

Even though I feel as if I am completely
on my own,
I needn't go through all this
difficult pain alone.
I'm telling every grieving father
and every grieving mother
That we stand tall
whenever we open our hearts to each other.

358

Within a Hebrew prayer for the dead, you'll find
Quite a useful rule of thumb:
Those who have passed echo within our hearts
and our minds,
And what they did is part
of what we have become.

359

We will—one day—take our very last breath.
This is no surprise or revelation,
But nature doesn't believe in death—
Only in transformation.

From the work of German scientist
Wernher von Braun

360

Standing alone as grief upon me does pour
Is bound to make my sorrow more,
But two together in distress
Will make our common sorrows less.

Based on a quote from Irish writer
Samuel Beckett

3 6 1

This raging storm of grief
in its thunder has caught me,
And I have no idea how I can become strong,
But as a famous rabbi has clearly taught me,
I will move slowly from tears to silence to song.

Based on teachings from the founder
of Hasidic Judaism, Rabbi Yisroel ben Eliezer
(often called Baal Shem Tov)

362

Aberration. Decimation.
Lamentation. Desolation.
Contemplation. Inspiration.
Reformation. Adaptation.

363

In order to manage and handle
The pain of grief's starkness,
It's better to light a candle
Than it is to curse the darkness.

Based on a Chinese proverb

3 6 4

Tender child, won't you tell me how
Through all this grief, I can more capably plow?
My lost daughter has now offered me
this demanding warning—
She insists that I grow
from the presence of mourning
to the presents of morning.

3 6 5

For my child's company,
I will certainly forever yearn,
But the strength and wisdom born of my pain
will begin to ease my fiery burn.
With grief's constant aching,
I'll become able to coexist
As I learn to make my way
through mourning's darkest mist.

Giving in Robin's Memory

What Robin found most upsetting about her illness was the fact that she didn't receive a proper diagnosis until many years after she first began to exhibit symptoms. She suffered great stress, anxiety, and depression from being told that nothing was wrong with her—a situation not uncommon among other such patients. In conjunction with Robin's beloved rheumatologist, Dr. Lisa Sammaritano, it was decided that the thrust of the investigations supported by the Robin Joy Sillau Memorial Research Fund for Connective Tissue Disease (you've read about that charitable endowment in the introductory section of this book) will be dedicated to finding ways for bringing the diagnosis of this malady closer to the onset of symptoms. Research will also be conducted to discover which therapies would be most effective in attempting to alleviate the various disturbing and painful attributes of Robin's illness and of others similar to it.

If you would like to make a contribution to our philanthropic effort, please make out a check payable to the Hospital for Special Surgery. On the memo line, please write the full name of the fund. Mail your check to the hospital at this address:

Hospital for Special Surgery
535 East 70th Street
New York, NY 10021

Robin and I take this opportunity to thank you for your kind generosity and for your wonderfully commendable willingness to share with others.

About the Author

Holly Snow Sillau, a graduate of New York University, has a bachelor of arts degree in mathematics and a master of arts degree in mathematical scholarship. She retired from the New York City Department of Education after teaching high school math for over thirty years. Throughout much of her long career, she coached other teachers on methodology and content. What most qualifies her to speak from the heart on the topics covered in *Through the Mourning Mist: 365 Poems of Validation and Encouragement*—and in her other three books—is the fact that as of January 2010, she is, and always will be, a bereaved parent.

28232662R00236

Made in the USA
Charleston, SC
05 April 2014